Interlacing Borders

More Than 100 Intricate Designs Made Easy

Donna Hussain

Credits

Editor-in-Chief ✍ Kerry I. Smith
Technical Editor ✍ Melissa A. Lowe
Managing Editor ✍ Judy Petry
Copy Editor ✍ Tina Cook
Design Director ✍ Cheryl Stevenson
Text Designer ✍ Kay Green
Cover Designer ✍ Jim Gerlitz
Illustrator ✍ Laurel Strand
Photographer ✍ Brent Kane

Interlacing Borders:
More Than 100 Intricate Designs Made Easy
© 1998 by Donna Hussain

MISSION STATEMENT

*We are dedicated to providing
quality products and service by
working together to inspire creativity
and to enrich the lives we touch.*

Martingale & Company
PO Box 118
Bothell, WA 98041-0118 USA

Printed in the United States of America
03 02 01 00 99   6 5 4 3 2

The information in this book is presented in good faith, but no warranty is given nor results guaranteed. Since Martingale & Company has no control over choice of materials or procedures, it assumes no responsibility for the use of this information.

Library of Congress Cataloging-in-Publication Data
Hussain, Donna.
    Interlacing borders : more than 100 intricate designs made easy / Donna Hussain.
        p. cm.
        ISBN 1-56477-237-3
        1. Patchwork—Patterns. 2. Quilting—Patterns. 3. Appliqué—Patterns. I. Title.
    TT835.H87 1998
    746.46'041—dc21   98-10348
                                                        CIP

CONTENTS

INTRODUCTION

My interest in interlacing patterns began with visits to India and Pakistan, where I fell in love with the intricate over-under designs adorning the walls of mosques and palaces. Immediately, I began planning a series of Islamic quilts that would feature these beautiful designs.

As I learned how to draw the designs and experimented with bias tubes, I collected patterns. Interlacing designs, I learned, are common in art throughout the world, from Roman mosaics to Celtic knotwork.

Cathedrals incorporated interlacing designs in their ornamentation. Artisans used them in stone lintels, wood-carved doors, tiled foyers, marble inlays, iron fences, and window grills. Today, you can find interlacing designs on jewelry, fabric trims, engravings, picture frames, fine china, greeting cards, and decorative plaques. This universality means that the designs are appropriate for quilts of all styles–enhancing both traditional and contemporary patchwork.

GETTING STARTED

The idea for this book was born when my quilting friends began to ask for my patterns and for tips on sewing the bias tubes. To get started, read the basics: how to draw interlacing patterns, how to plan and mark designs on fabric, how to make bias tubes, and how to appliqué bias tubes in interlacing designs. Then, choose from more than one hundred patterns for borders, sashing, blocks, or quilting.

Each pattern is provided on a grid. The advantages of using a grid are that you can easily increase or decrease the pattern to fit your quilt, and you can accurately reproduce the pattern on your fabric. To customize a pattern for your quilt, you simply adjust the size of the grid unit(s). As you look through the patterns on pages 23–63, you'll notice that each indicates a skill level, the number of bias tubes you need, and the number of grid units in the pattern. Some of the designs in this book are simple one-square patterns:

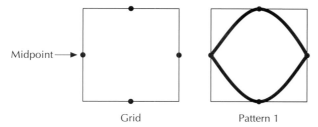

Midpoint →

Grid   Pattern 1

Notice that the grid has a dot at the midpoint of each side. To draw this pattern, you draw a grid with dots at the midpoints as shown, then connect the dots. Using a grid that is two units wide and two units deep (2 x 2), you can create a design like this:

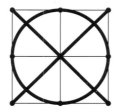

Using a grid that is four units wide and two units deep (4 x 2), you can create this design:

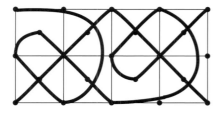

To create a border or sashing design, you repeat the basic pattern. Each pattern in this book shows several repetitions to help you visualize the finished design.

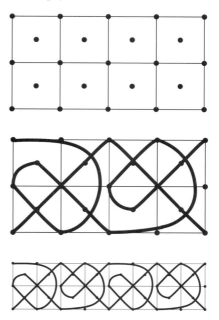

TIP

The patterns in this book are ordered according to sewing difficulty. Easy-to-sew patterns appear at the beginning; more challenging patterns follow.

DRAWING GRIDS AND PATTERNS

It's a good idea to practice drawing the grids and patterns before you work on fabric. For the exercises that follow, get out a pencil and draw directly on the grids in this book.

Exercise 1

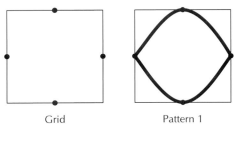

Grid   Pattern 1

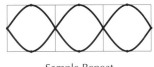

Sample Repeat

1. Connect the dots in Grid A to draw the pattern.

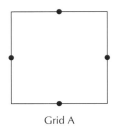

Grid A

2. Connect the dots in Grid B and draw repetitions of the pattern.

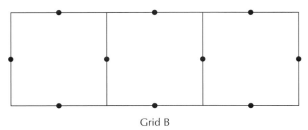

Grid B

Exercise 2

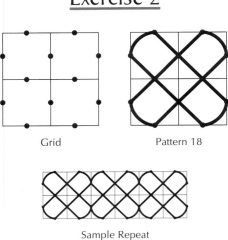

Grid   Pattern 18

Sample Repeat

1. Connect the dots in Grid C to draw the pattern.

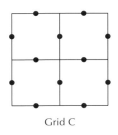

Grid C

2. Mark dots in Grid D and draw repetitions of the pattern.

Grid D

Exercise 3

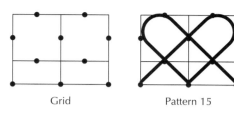

Grid   Pattern 15

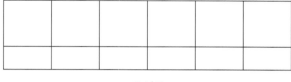

Sample Repeat

1. Connect the dots in Grid E to draw the pattern.

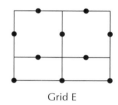

Grid E

2. Mark dots in Grid F and draw repetitions of the pattern.

Grid F

Exercise 4

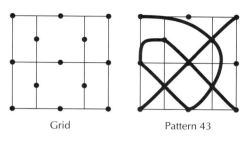

Grid   Pattern 43

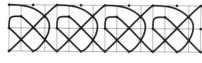

Sample Repeat

1. Mark dots in Grid G, as shown above, then connect the dots to draw the pattern. The pattern will not touch every dot.

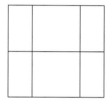

Grid G

2. Mark dots in Grid H and draw repetitions of the pattern. This pattern starts with a half-unit, so leave half of the first unit in Grid H blank.

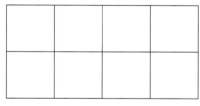

Grid H

Exercise 5

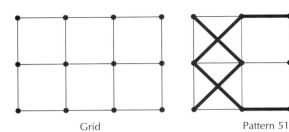

Grid

Pattern 51

Sample Repeat

2. Mark dots in Grid J and draw repetitions of the pattern.

Grid J

3. On a piece of paper, draw 3 horizontal lines, spacing them 1" apart. To complete the grid, add vertical lines spaced 1" apart. Mark dots in the grid and draw repetitions of the pattern.

1. Mark dots in Grid I, as shown above, then connect the dots to draw the pattern.

Grid I

CHOOSING BACKGROUND FABRIC

There are a few important guidelines for choosing background fabric to use with interlacing designs.

∽ The background and bias-tube fabrics should contrast in value. For example, if you choose a light fabric for your background, use medium or dark fabrics for your bias tubes.

∽ Grid lines should be easy to see. A solid color or tone-on-tone fabric is much easier to work with than a print.

TIP

Choose a marking pen or pencil that will show up well on the background fabric and be easy to remove. My favorite markers are a blue chemical pen (wash lines away with cold water) and white or silver quilter's pencils (wash lines away with a toothbrush and soap). Whatever marker you choose, test it before you mark your borders. Draw sample lines on a small piece of your background fabric, then make sure you can remove them.

The step-by-step instructions in this section are meant for borders, but you can also use the designs for sashing, blocks, and quilting. You draw the patterns on fabric the same way, but you may need to adjust the grid-unit size. For example, you would need a smaller grid unit for narrow sashing than for wide quilt borders.

Design Size

Before you can cut borders or transfer your pattern to fabric, you need to estimate the finished width and length of your borders. Don't worry about exact border measurements (based on your quilt top) at this stage. The decision to make now is grid and pattern size. Suppose you want to use Pattern 29:

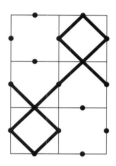

Pattern 29

The grid for Pattern 29 is three units deep (2 x 3). The depth of the grid is the basis for calculating border width. For example, if you choose a grid of 1" squares, the border will be 3" wide (3 x 1). If you want a border that is wider (or narrower) than 3", enlarge (or reduce) your grid unit. A grid of 1¼" squares would make the border design 3¾" wide (3 x 1¼); a grid of ½" squares would make the border design 1½" wide (3 x ½).

TIP

The depth of your pattern (number of grid units deep) times the grid-unit size determines the width of your border design. The size of your quilt determines the length of your border.

To make the interlacing design, you repeat the pattern along the length of the border strip. The number of repeats depends on the size of your quilt. Most quilts have a partial pattern, not a complete repeat, at the ends of the borders.

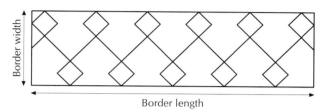

Border width

Border length

TIP

For most quilts, grid units should be no smaller than ½" square and no larger than 2" square. Make your grid units ½", ¾", 1", 1¼", 1½", 1¾", or 2" square. Keeping to quarter-inch increments simplifies measuring and drawing grids on fabric.

In my classes, I recommend a grid of 1¼" squares and ¼"-wide bias tubes for students making their first bias-tube borders. Sewing curves and angles is simple on a grid this size, and the tube is easy to handle and appropriate to the scale of the grid.

Side Borders

Once you've chosen a pattern and grid size, you are ready to prepare the side borders.

Fabric width: Cut your fabric 6" wider than the depth of your chosen design. For example, if your pattern depth is 3 units and you're using a grid of 1" squares, cut your side borders 9" wide: (3 x 1) + 6 = 9. The extra fabric is for seam allowances, handling convenience, distortion that may occur when you stitch the bias tubes, and design margins. You will trim the border strips to size later (see page 17).

Fabric length: Measure the length of your quilt sides. If one side is longer than the other, determine the average measurement of the two. Add 6" to this figure. The total is how long you need to cut your side border strips. Again, you will trim the strips later.

Marking Borders

Mark the side borders, following the steps below. This method ensures that you can center your interlacing design on your quilt and allows you to postpone deciding how to handle the corners. It's easier to decide how to finish the corners after you have partially sewn your borders. Corner options are discussed on pages 14–15.

1. Suppose you chose Pattern 29, with a grid of 1¼" squares. Note that the grid has four horizontal lines. Using a ruler and marking pen or pencil, draw the horizontal grid lines, 1¼" apart, roughly centering them on your border strip.

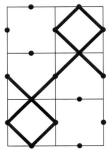

Pattern 29
on 1¼" x 1¼" grid

2. Draw the vertical lines on your border strip, 1¼" apart, to complete the grid.

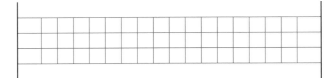

3. Mark the midpoint dots on your border fabric. Be sure to use a ruler to mark the dots accurately.

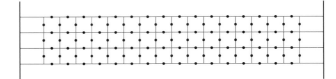

4. Connect the dots as illustrated for the pattern, working out from the center of the border strip.

Start here.

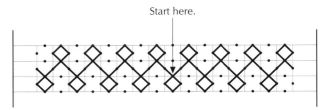

5. Repeat steps 1–4 to mark your second side border strip.

Top and Bottom Borders

Cut your top and bottom borders the same width as your side borders. To calculate the length of the top and bottom borders, use the following formula:

width of the quilt through its center +
(2 x the width of the side borders) + 6"

Mark your top and bottom borders, following the previous instructions for marking side borders.

Bias Tubes

A bias tube begins with a strip of fabric that is cut on the bias. Why cut on the bias? Because bias strips stretch. In most patchwork, fabric is cut on the straight of grain to avoid any stretching, so that quilt blocks come out square. But when you make curved designs like those in this book, stretching is a plus. Because bias tubes stretch, you can sew them into curves and circles without creating puckers.

I recommend using bias bars, available at most fabric and quilt stores, to make bias tubes. You sew the bias tubes right side out, then press the seam so it is on the back of the tube. The bias-tube method is much easier than sewing narrow strips together, then struggling to turn the strips right side out.

Bias bars range from ⅛" to 2" wide. The size of the bias bar determines the width of the bias tube: a ¼"-wide bias bar makes a ¼"-wide finished bias tube.

To decide which bias-tube size is appropriate for your quilt, make a sample of one or two repetitions of your pattern on a piece of muslin. Sew the design, using ¼" bias tubes. Audition the design by placing it next to your quilt top. If the design line looks too thin, use wider bias tubes. If the design line looks too thick, use narrower bias tubes.

TIP

Be sure to choose a fabric that gives when pulled on the bias. Because they do not stretch easily, densely woven fabrics like pima cotton and batiks are less suitable for bias tubes than more loosely woven cottons.

Cutting Bias Strips

1. To make a bias tube, start with an 18" x 18" or larger piece of fabric. Be sure to square up the fabric so that grain lines run horizontally and vertically. Align the 45°-angle mark on your cutting guide with the upper edge of the fabric. Using a rotary cutter, make a bias cut.

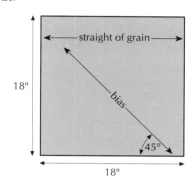

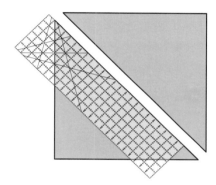

2. Measuring from the bias-cut edge, cut strips for bias tubes. The size of the bias bar determines the strip width. Here is a helpful rule of thumb:

strip width =
(bias-bar width x 2) + ½" (for the seam allowances)

For example, if you're using a ¼"-wide bias bar, cut 1"-wide strips: (¼" x 2) + ½" = 1"

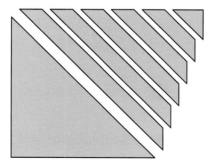

TIP
For straight-line patterns like Pattern 2 on page 26, you can cut strips on the straight of grain rather than on the bias, if desired.

Sewing Bias Tubes

1. Fold each bias strip in half lengthwise, wrong sides together. Press.

2. Raise your sewing-machine needle to the up position. Place your bias bar in a folded, pressed bias strip. Place the bar and strip under the presser foot, aligning the fold with the outer edge of the foot. Adjust the needle position to the right or left as necessary to encase the bias bar snugly.
3. Once the needle position is set, remove the bias bar. Sew the length of the folded strip, keeping the fold aligned with the presser-foot edge.

NOTE: If you can't adjust the needle position on your sewing machine, move the folded strip to the right or left of the presser-foot edge until the needle encases the bias bar snugly. Remove the bias bar. As you sew, try to keep the same distance from the fold to the edge of the presser foot.

4. Re-insert the bias bar into the sewn tube. Trim the raw edges $\frac{1}{16}$" from the stitching line.

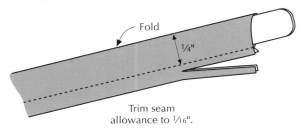

Fold

$\frac{1}{4}$"

Trim seam
allowance to $\frac{1}{16}$".

5. Twist the seam to the middle of the bias bar. With the bar in the tube, press the seam allowance to one side. (Metal bias bars heat up when pressed, which helps press the seam flat and creases the folds of the tube.)

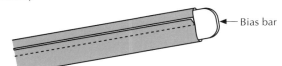

Bias bar

6. Remove the bias bar and press the tube again, once with the seam side up, once with the seam side down.

TIP
Use lightweight thread to reduce seam bulk and help keep the tubes from puckering when you appliqué them in curves.

Grid Dots—Critical Accuracy Points

In patchwork, quilters learn where sewing accuracy is critical. For example, the points of triangles and diamonds in adjoining blocks should meet. In interlacing designs, sewing *accuracy is critical at the grid dots*. The dots are more important than the pattern lines, which merely tell you which grid dot comes next. The grid dots indicate bias-tube placement.

If you want your design to look precisely rather than carelessly sewn, follow these guidelines.

✎ Center bias tubes over grid dots wherever two tubes cross (crossover points).

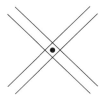

✎ When appliquéing angles or curves within a design where no crossover occurs, the outer edge of the tube should touch the dot, not be centered over it.

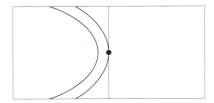

✎ The bias-tube design must stay within the grid. When appliquéing angles or curves at the edge of a border design, the outer edge of the tube should just touch dots on the perimeter of the grid, not be centered over them.

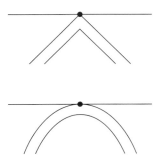

A special set of sewing instructions applies to patterns that have horizontal and vertical lines (no diagonals or curves). Patterns 12, 14, 16, 17, 21, 30, 45, 47, 49, 50, 53, 87, 88, 91, and 92 belong to this group. The primary objective in sewing these patterns is to appliqué the tubes in straight lines.

∾ Align bias tubes below horizontal grid lines.

∾ Align bias tubes to the right of vertical grid lines.

Angles do not always turn at a dot. Instead, the alignment of the tubes on the grid determines where the angle turns. This will become obvious to you as you sew.

Appliquéing Bias Tubes

Match thread to the bias tube, not the background fabric.

1. Begin in the middle of your border design, where two lines cross. Place the middle section of one tube (not an end) over one line of the cross, seam side down. *Center the tube over the dot at the intersection. This is a critical accuracy point.*

2. Holding the tube in place with your thumb (or with a pin), appliqué through the intersection, sewing a section about 1" long. It is not necessary to sew both sides of the bias tube; you can appliqué the second edge later.

   Most of the designs in this book do not require pinning. You can hold the tube in place with your thumb as you stitch from dot to dot. Some people are more comfortable using pins, so if you prefer to pin, be sure to pin only a small section at a time. Pins can snag and pull your thread as you appliqué. You can also apply a light coat of gluestick to the tube, finger press it to the background fabric, then appliqué.

3. Place a second tube over the first at the intersection of the pattern lines. This crossover (one tube under, one tube over) creates the interlacing look of these patterns. Holding the second tube in place with your thumb (or with a pin), appliqué through the intersection, sewing a section about 1" long. Be

sure to center the tube over the dot at the intersection. This first crossover sets up the over-under sequence.

4. Continue appliquéing the edge of the tube, following these instructions for:

   Angles: Miter the tube at the point of the angle. As you approach the angle dot, sew along the outside edge of the bias tube. When you reach the dot, backstitch or make a knot to secure the tube. Then fold the tube at the appropriate angle and continue to appliqué along the outer edge of the tube. When you appliqué the second edge of the tube (inside the angle), use your fingernail to push the edge into a tuck. Stitch the tuck in place.

   Curves: Bias tubes form curves easily. If necessary, pin the curve to hold the tube in place. Appliqué the inner edge of the curve first. Take small stitches along tight curves. Minimize puckers by pressing the inner edge with your thumb as you sew. Stretch the outer edge of the tube to make it lie flat when you appliqué.

   Crossovers: Crossovers occur whenever two bias tubes intersect. To check the sequence (which tube should be under and which should be over), look at the last crossover. If a tube was under last, it will be over in the next crossover, or vice versa.

   At crossovers, I prefer to sew the bottom tube first. If I reach a crossover while sewing the top tube and find no bottom tube in position, I have two options: I can stop sewing until I've appliquéd the bottom tube, or I can leave a section of the top tube temporarily unsewn at the crossover, creating a gap, and continue sewing. Later, I can pull the bottom tube through the gap and appliqué it in place.

   When Pattern Lines Meet Without Crossing: In some patterns, different lines meet at a grid dot without actually crossing. Place each bias tube just short of the grid dot so that the tubes do not touch. The background fabric, showing through the gap between the two tubes, will accent the design lines.

Ending: The best place to end is under a crossover so you can hide the raw edge of the tube. Appliqué to the crossover dot. Do not trim any excess until you have stitched one side of the top tube. The stitches help secure the ending tube.

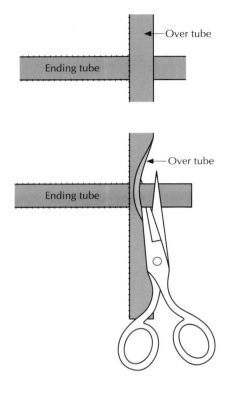

Adding a Length or New Color of Bias Tube: Ideally, the end of one tube and the start of the next will butt against one another under a crossover. To end a tube, follow the directions above. Pin the new tube at the correct angle over the tubes at the crossover. Secure the new tube with several stitches before you trim the tube and hide the cut end under the top tube.

These designs are easy to stitch because there are no raw edges to turn under. Your stitches do not need to be as small as traditional appliqué stitches.

To hand appliqué: Bring your needle up through the background fabric, catching the edge of the folded tube. Bring the needle down through the background fabric only, as shown.

Make short, straight stitches.

To machine appliqué: Carefully baste curved designs before appliquéing them to avoid puckers and keep curves symmetrical. Straight-line designs require no basting. Align the edges of tubes with grid lines as you appliqué.

Finishing Corners

Deciding how to finish your corners can be a challenge. I've found that the best approach is to partially complete the borders, then tackle the corners. When I reach this point, I lay my borders next to my quilt and play with possible corner treatments to see what works best. Here are a few alternatives:

∽ Sew the ends of your bias tubes into border seams. In most cases, you will not be able to complete an entire repetition of your pattern at the end of your border. It doesn't matter if you have a partial pattern at the seams.

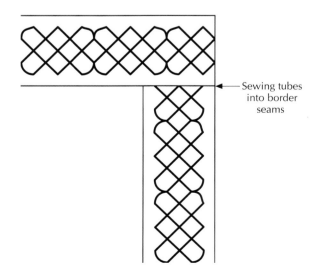

Sewing tubes into border seams

✎ Close your border designs. Tuck the tube ends into the design in an under position.

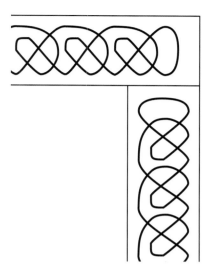

✎ Round the corners. Join the ends of bias tubes in the top and bottom borders to the side border designs. Try to incorporate design elements from the border pattern when turning the corner. In some cases, you may choose to join only one tube; in other cases, all tubes.

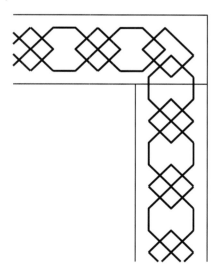

✎ Bring tube ends into corners and hide them under an appliquéd element, such as a flower, or hide them in the seams of a corner block.

✎ Treat the corners independently. Add another bias design, or quilt the area in a complementary design.

Practice Pattern

It's a good idea to practice sewing tubes before you work on your quilt. As you stitch this practice pattern, you'll encounter most of the challenges of bias-tube appliqué. Once you've completed this exercise, you will be ready to add interlacing designs to your own quilts.

1. Cut a 6" x 12" strip of muslin.
2. With a marking pen or pencil, draw three horizontal lines on the muslin, 1¼" apart. Add 7 vertical lines 1¼" apart to make a grid. Add dots at each intersection and at the center of each square, then connect the dots as shown to make the pattern.

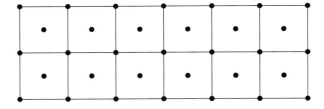

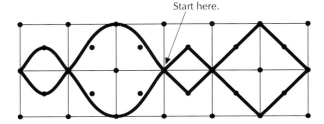

Start here.

3. Make several different-colored ¼"-wide bias tubes, following the instructions on page 11.
4. Appliqué the tubes, following the pattern on your muslin. Remember to begin at a crossover in the middle of the design. Referring to step 4 on pages 13–14, practice appliquéing angles, curves, and crossovers. At one of the crossovers, change to a new tube color.

Deciding when to add borders to your quilt depends on personal preference and the corner treatment you choose. Here are some factors to consider:

∽ Appliquéing border strips and blocks is less cumbersome than appliquéing an entire quilt top.

∽ If you intend to sew the bias-tube ends into border seams, you must finish the appliqué before sewing the borders to your quilt top.

∽ If you plan to round the corners, you must attach the borders to your quilt top before finishing the appliqué.

You need to trim excess fabric before sewing the border design to your quilt top. Don't forget that the border strips are cut wider than the desired finished size (see "Design Size" on page 9). How wide do you want the finished border to be? Do you want a margin of border fabric around the design, or do you want your design to touch the seams?

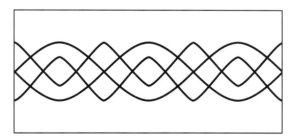

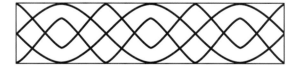

Use a marking pen or pencil and a ruler to draw lines at the edges of the design as shown. Next, draw lines parallel to the design-edge lines to mark your desired margins around the design—these are the stitching lines. Draw lines ¼" from the stitching lines to mark seam allowances. You will trim the borders on the seam-allowance lines.

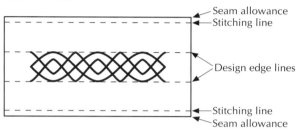

Make sure that your designs are centered, parallel sides are alike, and ends match before trimming border length. Take a break to think about your choices before you take scissors or rotary cutter in hand. After all that appliqué, it's a good idea to be sure before you trim!

Three Different Approaches

Adding interlacing designs to a quilt is fun and fairly easy. Walk through my approaches to three different quilts, all featuring the Sawtooth Star block.

Each approach is a bit different. In the first example, Star Quilt A, the top, including borders, is pieced before the interlacing designs are added. In the second example, Star Quilt B, the bias tubes are appliquéd to border strips, then the strips are joined to the quilt top. In the final example, Star Quilt C, the designs are appliquéd on blocks, then the blocks are pieced into a quilt top.

Star Quilt A

For Star Quilt A, I chose a straight border design that would both frame and draw the viewer's eye to the patchwork.

Pattern 21 • *Easy* • 2 tubes

This easy pattern, which enhances both patchwork and appliqué quilts, is meant to be used in the corners of the border with connecting bias tubes between the corner designs. I find that the best approach for this type of design is to sew the tube design after the borders have been attached to the quilt top. In this example, my quilt borders are cut 6½" wide.

After sewing the borders to my quilt, I draw five horizontal lines, each 1" apart and parallel to the border seam lines. Notice how these lines cross at the corners, creating a grid that is four squares wide and four squares deep (4 x 4).

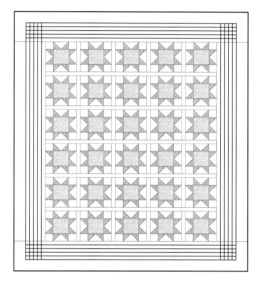

Next, I mark dots on the corner grids, then draw the design by connecting the appropriate dots. Each corner grid contains the same design turned in a different direction. Finally, I draw straight lines to connect the corner patterns.

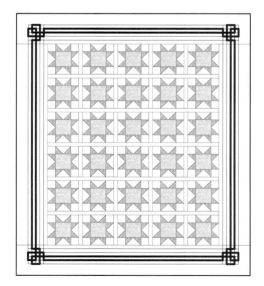

The corners include several crossovers, where I can add tubes if necessary. To determine the length needed for the long connecting tubes, I measure my quilt from corner design to corner design. I may have to join two or more fabric strips to be sure my bias tube is long enough.

TIP

A seam in a bias tube adds bulk, reducing the tube's ability to stretch and make turns and angles. For this reason, bias tubes should be made from a single bias strip of fabric. To add length, you usually start a new tube segment at a crossover. In Star Quilt A, however, the interlacing patterns are far apart. A seamed bias tube may be necessary for a large quilt because there are no crossovers to hide the introduction of a new tube segment.

As I appliqué, I arrange each bias tube so one edge touches the grid lines, as shown. This approach ensures that the tubes lie straight.

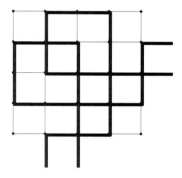

Star Quilt B

For Star Quilt B, I chose a curving, interlacing border design.
For large quilts, it's easiest to appliqué this type of design to border strips,
then join the strips to the quilt top.

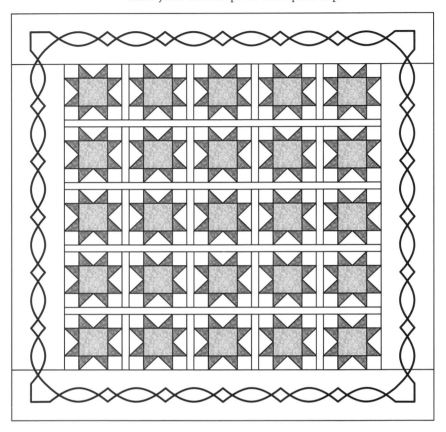

Pattern 10 • *Easy* • 2 tubes

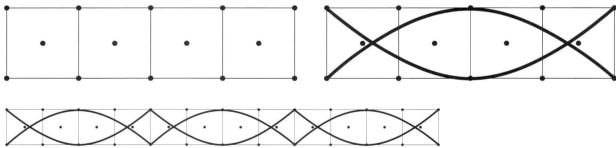

The grid for this design is 4 x 1, or four squares wide and one square deep. In this example, I want a 1½"-wide border design with 2"-wide margins. Adding ½" for seam allowances, my unfinished borders will be 6" wide when trimmed (1½ + 2 + 2 + ½ = 6). At this stage, however, I want to work with wider fabric for handling convenience. So I add another 6" to the border, cutting my borders 12" wide (6 + 6 = 12).

To determine how long to cut my side border strips, I measure my quilt and add 6". To cut my top and bottom borders, I apply the formula on page 10.

After cutting the border strips, I draw two parallel lines 1½" apart, centering the lines on the border fabric as shown. Then I draw vertical lines 1½" apart to finish the grid.

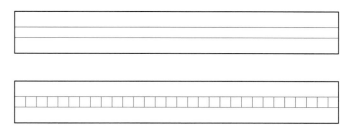

Next, I mark dots as illustrated in the pattern. I draw the interlacing design by connecting the appropriate dots, starting from the center of the border and working outward.

I appliqué the interlacing bias tubes as described on pages 13–14. Because I plan to round the corners of my quilt, I end my appliqué about 7" from the border ends, leaving the border design incomplete and the bias-tube ends loose. (Later, I will use these tubes to turn the corner.) I trim the borders to size and stitch them to the quilt. To finish, I draw the corner grid and pattern and complete the appliqué.

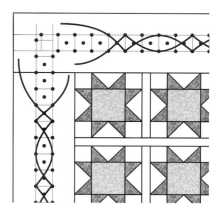

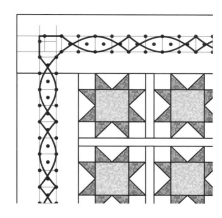

Star Quilt C

For Star Quilt C, I chose to alternate Sawtooth Star blocks
with an easy interlacing block design based on a 2 x 2 grid of squares.

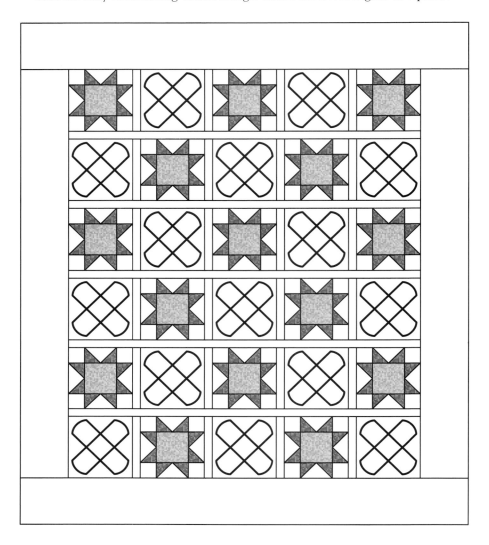

Pattern 18 • *Easy* • 2 tubes

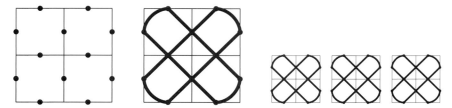

To determine the size of my interlacing blocks, I measure my unfinished patchwork blocks. The background fabric for my interlacing blocks should be cut the same size as the patchwork blocks. In this example, my unfinished blocks are 8½" square.

I want my interlacing design to be slightly smaller than the Sawtooth Stars, so I use a grid of 3½" squares. This gives me a 7" x 7" interlacing design.

I mark the center of each background block, then draw the grid and mark the midpoint dots as shown.

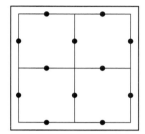

After connecting the appropriate dots, I follow the instructions on pages 13–14 for appliquéing the interlacing bias tubes. To finish, I assemble the quilt top as illustrated on page 22, alternating the star and interlacing blocks in every row.

As you can see from the gallery of quilts on pages 29–36, there are many ways to use interlacing designs. This section describes some creative variations for the patterns. Experiment and come up with designs of your own.

Change Color and Value: Play with color. Choose a single color for the bias tubes in your design, or make each tube a different color. Try making each pattern repetition a new color, or piece the border background with a variety of fabrics. I like to use a single border fabric that gradually changes in value from dark to light, as in "Quintessential Quilter's Round Robin" on page 36 and "Forest Light" on page 31.

Change Curves to Angles or Angles to Curves: Try changing the basic pattern shape. Note how the following pattern has a completely different look when the curves change to angles.

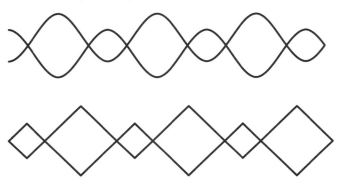

Mix Curves and Angles: Make several repetitions of the pattern with curves, then several with angles.

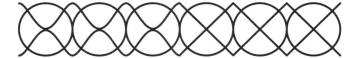

Change the Scale: Grid size can alter the look of a pattern. So can the shape of the grid units. Try using rectangles instead of squares or changing the scale of the grid.

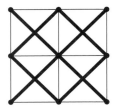
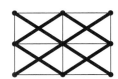

Mix Bias-Tube Widths: Vary the width of the bias tubes in your design. For example, use a ¼" bias tube for one design line and a ⅜" bias tube for another.

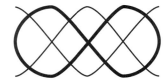

Fill in Interlacing Designs: Fill spaces inside the designs with fabric that contrasts with the background fabric, as in Cathedral Windows designs.

Use Interlacing Designs as Sashing:

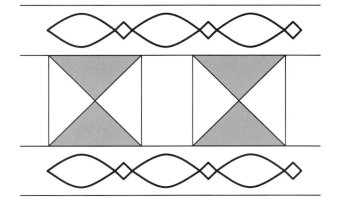

Alternate Patchwork Blocks with Interlacing Design Blocks:

Separate Repetitions of Interlacing Designs with Straight Lines:

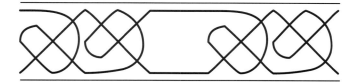

Make Stand-Alone Designs: Many of the patterns in this book are independent units. They can be repeated side by side in borders, placed in corners, or set midpoint in borders.

Make an Irregular Grid: The units within a grid can vary in size and shape. And grids can be any shape you choose.

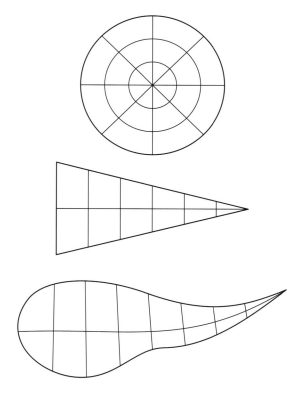

Combine Patterns:

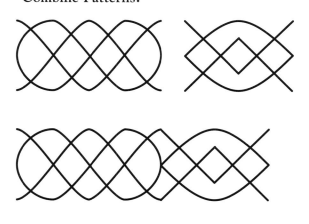

TIP

Use interlacing designs for hand or machine quilting patterns. Draw the appropriate grid and pattern on your quilt, then stitch.

Pattern 1 • *Easy* • 2 tubes

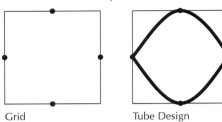

Grid   Tube Design   Sample Repeat

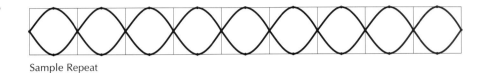

Pattern 2 • *Easy* • 2 tubes

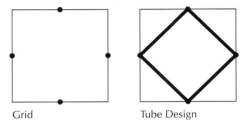

Grid   Tube Design   Sample Repeat

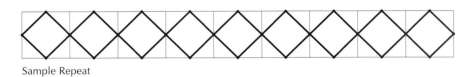

Pattern 3 • *Easy* • 2 tubes

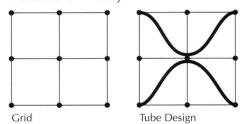

Grid   Tube Design   Sample Repeat

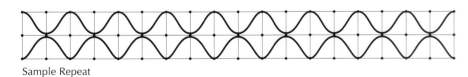

Because the bias tubes in this design don't cross, there's no place
to hide tube ends. Make your bias tubes the full border length,
then hide the ends in the border seams.

Pattern 4 • *Easy* • 2 tubes

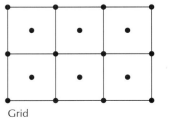

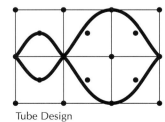

Grid   Tube Design   Sample Repeat

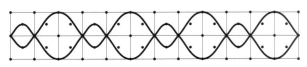

Pattern 5 • *Easy* • 2 tubes

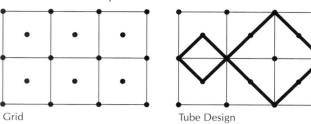

Grid

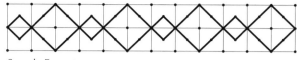

Tube Design   Sample Repeat

Pattern 6 • *Easy* • 2 tubes

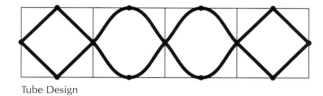

Grid   Tube Design

Sample Repeat

Pattern 7 • *Easy* • 2 tubes

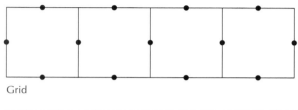

Grid   Tube Design   Sample Repeat

Pattern 8 • *Easy* • 2 tubes

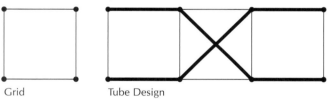

Grid   Tube Design

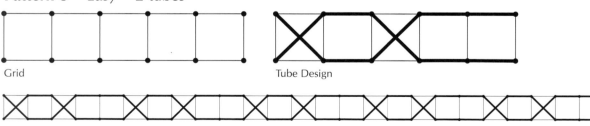

Sample Repeat

Pattern 9 • *Easy* • 2 tubes

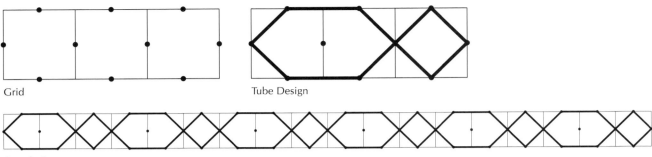

Grid

Tube Design

Sample Repeat

Pattern 10 • *Easy* • 2 tubes

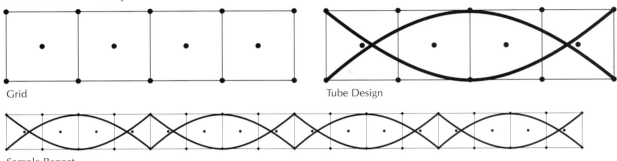

Grid

Tube Design

Sample Repeat

Pattern 11 • *Easy* • 2 tubes

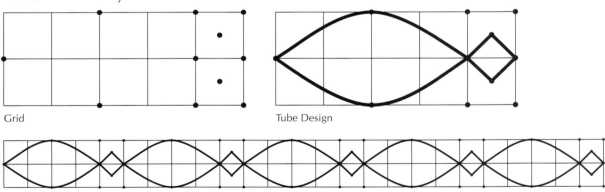

Grid

Tube Design

Sample Repeat

TRIBUTE TO GRANDMOTHER

By the Quintessential Quilters: Nancy Barrow, Ouida Braithwaite, Ann Brasher, Judy Denney, Antoinette Hine, Donna Hussain, Kit La Due, Joyce Moldenhauer, Teri Moore, Alice Morgan, Cynthia Mosby, Sandy Ross, Ruth Schindler, and Caroline Strauch; 1997, Sacramento, California, 63" x 83"; quilted by Donna Hussain. This quilt was inspired by a quilt in Judy Schroeder Tomlonson's book *Mennonite Quilts and Pieces* and by Lee Cleland's book *Quilting Makes the Quilt*. The inner border design is Pattern 78.

TWINKLE, TWINKLE, LITTLE HEARTS

By Candy Kraft, 1997, Vacaville, California, 45" x 45". This quilt was inspired by Alice Berg, Mary Ellen Von Holt, and Sylvia Johnson's book *Little Quilts—All Through the House*. The hearts are Pattern 15.

MIKE'S STREET

By Caroline Strauch, 1997, Sacramento, California, 17" x 21". Caroline made this quilt from a kit she purchased from The Fabric Patch in Montclair, California, using paper-piecing designs from Granny Nanny's Quilting Gadgets in Williamsburg, Virginia. The border design is Pattern 12.

FOURPATCH PLUS
By Donna Hussain, 1997, Sacramento, California, 36" x 53". The outer border design is Pattern 65, with curves instead of angles.

FOREST LIGHT
By Donna Hussain, 1997, Sacramento, California, 33" x 33". The side border is a variation of Pattern 73.

WIND SONG
By Donna Hussain, 1997, Sacramento, California, 39" x 42". The side border design is Pattern 43.

TRAVELING STAR OF THE EAST
By Donna Quartier, 1997, North Highlands, California, 74" x 88"; quilted by Donna Quartier and Jane Foster. The outer border design is Pattern 98.

EXOTIC PUZZLE
By Elizabeth Lonnquist, 1997, Colorado Springs, Colorado, 43" x 60". This quilt pattern is from Jackie Robinson's book *Tesselations*. The outer border design is Pattern 72.

A SWIRL OF CROWNS
By Donna Hussain, 1997, Sacramento, California, 33" x 39". The center design is Pattern 44. The border quilting echoes the interlacing design.

CAROUSEL HORSE
By Elfrieda DeLany, 1996, Sacramento, California, 42" x 39". This quilt, designed by Royal and Elfrieda DeLany, is embellished with Pattern 10.

MEMORIES OF MOROCCO
By Ruth Schindler and her quilt circle (Nancy Barrow, Antoinette Hine, Teri Moore, Cynthia Mosby, and Sandy Ross), 1997, Carmichael, California, 48" x 48". Patterns 16 and 33 appear in this quilt.

RAINBOW WEAVING

By Elizabeth Lonnquist, 1997, Colorado Springs, Colorado, 51" x 64". This quilt pattern is from Blanche Young's book *Nine Patch Wonders*. The border design is a variation of Pattern 95, with rectangles instead of squares.

STARBURST FUN

By Joyce Reece, 1997, Carmichael, California, 35" x 35". This quilt is based on the designs and techniques described in Camille Remme's book *Starburst Mosaic*. The border design is Pattern 55.

QUINTESSENTIAL QUILTER'S ROUND ROBIN

By Ouida Braithwaite and her quilt circle (Nancy Barrow, Donna Hussain, Kit La Due, and Sandy Ross), 1997, Sacramento, California, 69" x 69"; quilted by Ouida Braithwaite. The inner border design is a variation of Pattern 59.

LEAVES IN THE WIND

By Cynthia Mosby, 1997, Carmichael, California, 42" x 38". This quilt is based on Vicky Lawrence's Autumn Cascade pattern, available through Prairie's Edge Patchwork in Overbrook, Kansas. The border design is Pattern 60.

Pattern 12 • *Easy* • 1 tube

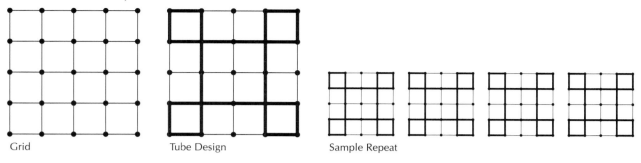

Grid   Tube Design   Sample Repeat

Pattern 13 • *Easy* • 1 tube per arch

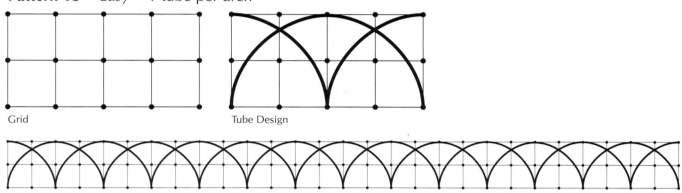

Grid   Tube Design

Sample Repeat

Sew tube ends into border, block, or sashing seams.

Pattern 14 • *Easy* • 1 tube

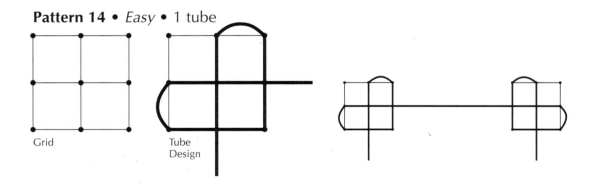

Grid   Tube Design

Pattern 15 • *Easy* • 1 tube

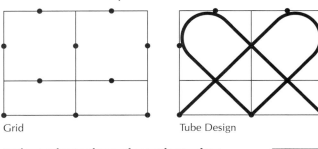

Grid

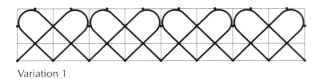

Tube Design

Variation 1

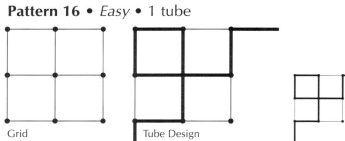

Variation 2

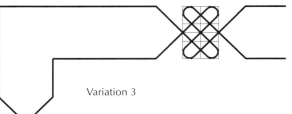

Variation 3

Pattern 16 • *Easy* • 1 tube

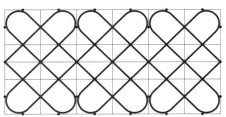

Grid　　　　　Tube Design

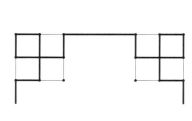

Pattern 17 • *Easy* • 2 tubes

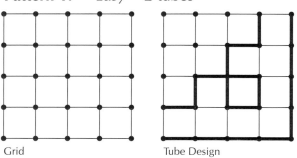

Grid　　　　　Tube Design

Pattern 18 • *Easy* • 2 tubes

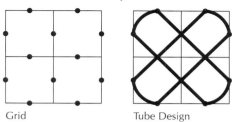

Grid   Tube Design

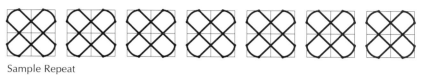

Sample Repeat

Pattern 19 • *Easy* • 1 tube

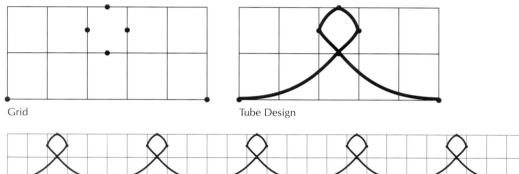

Grid   Tube Design

Sample Repeat

Pattern 20 • *Easy* • 2 tubes

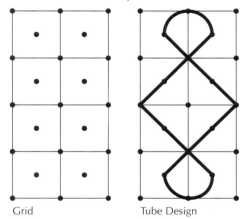

Grid   Tube Design   Sample Repeat

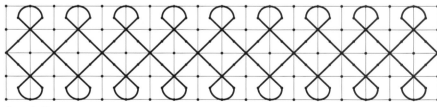

Pattern 21 • *Easy* • 2 tubes

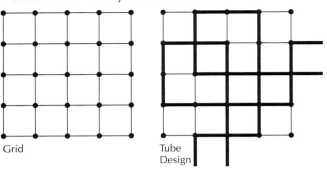

Grid

Tube
Design

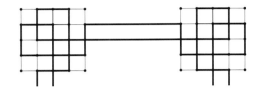

Pattern 22 • *Moderate* • 3 tubes

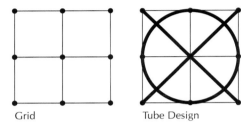

Grid

Tube Design

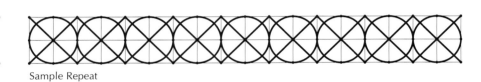

Sample Repeat

Pattern 23 • *Moderate* • 3 tubes

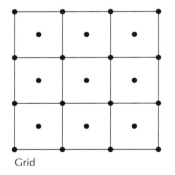

Grid

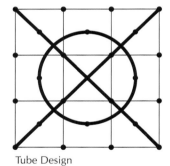

Tube Design

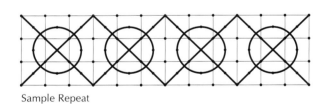

Sample Repeat

Pattern 24 • *Moderate* • 2 tubes

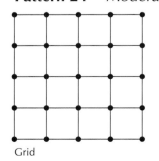

Grid

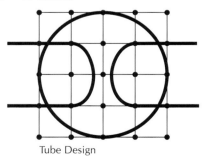

Tube Design

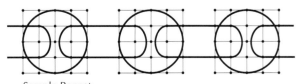

Sample Repeat

Pattern 25 • *Moderate* • 3 tubes

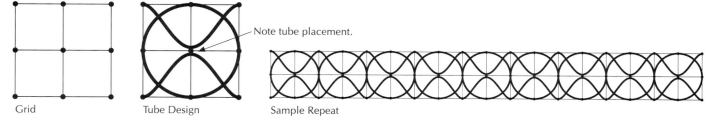

Grid

Tube Design — Note tube placement.

Sample Repeat

Pattern 26 • *Moderate* • 1 tube per brick

Grid

Tube Design

End here, under crossover.

Start here, under crossover.

Sample Repeat

Pattern 27 • *Moderate* • 1 tube

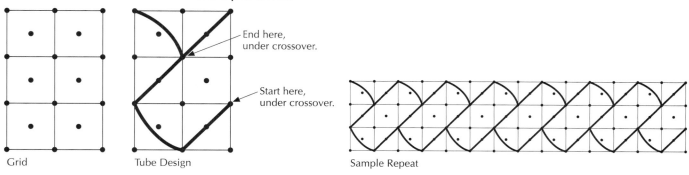

Grid

Tube Design

Pattern 28 • *Moderate* • 1 tube

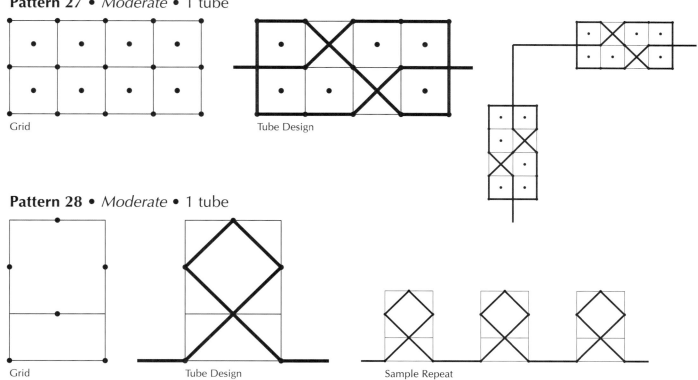

Grid

Tube Design

Sample Repeat

Pattern 29 • *Moderate* • 1 tube

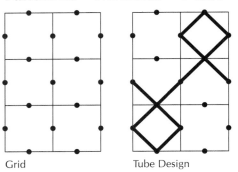

Grid

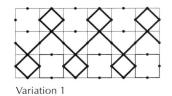

Tube Design

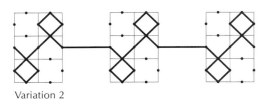

Variation 1   Variation 2

Pattern 30 • *Moderate* • 1 tube

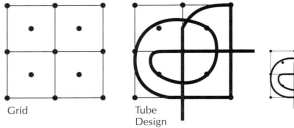

Grid

Tube
Design

Pattern 31 • *Moderate* • 3 tubes

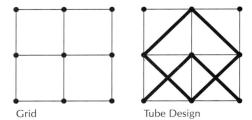

Grid   Tube Design

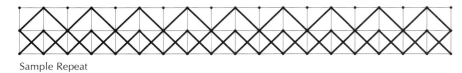

Sample Repeat

Pattern 32 • *Moderate* • 2 tubes

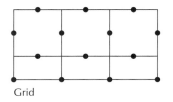

Grid   Tube Design

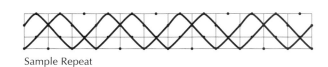

Sample Repeat

Pattern 33 • *Moderate* • 1 tube

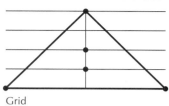

Grid

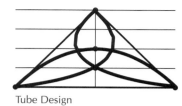

Tube Design

Sample Repeat

Pattern 34 • *Moderate* • 1 tube

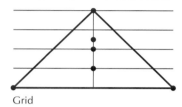

Grid

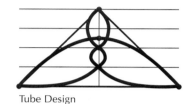

Tube Design

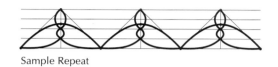

Sample Repeat

Pattern 35 • *Moderate* • 1 tube

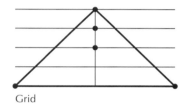

Grid

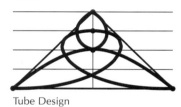

Tube Design

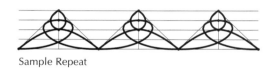

Sample Repeat

Pattern 36 • *Moderate* • 1 tube

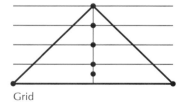

Grid

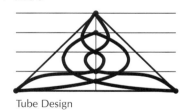

Tube Design

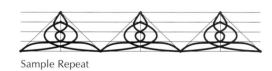

Sample Repeat

Pattern 37 • *Moderate* • 2 tubes

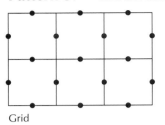

Grid

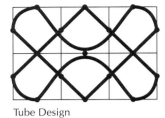

Tube Design

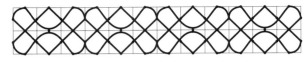

Sample Repeat

Pattern 38 • *Moderate* • 2 tubes

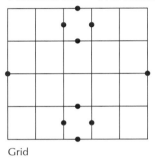

Grid

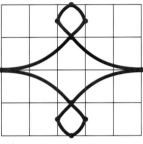

Tube Design

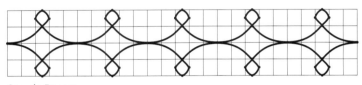

Sample Repeat

Pattern 39 • *Moderate* • 2 tubes

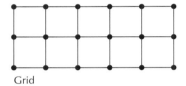

Grid

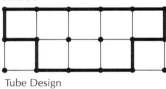

Tube Design

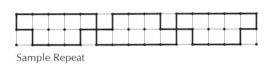

Sample Repeat

Alternate the direction of the pattern when repeating the design.

Pattern 40 • *Moderate* • 2 tubes

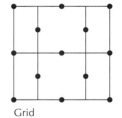

Grid

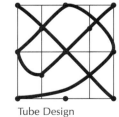

Tube Design

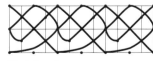

Variation 1

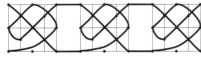

Variation 2

Pattern 41 • *Moderate* • 2 tubes

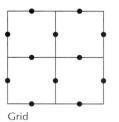

Grid

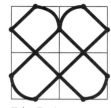

Tube Design

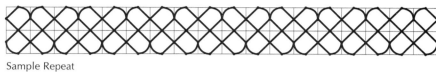

Sample Repeat

Pattern 42 • *Moderate* • 4 tubes

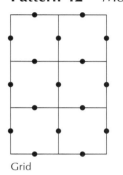

Grid

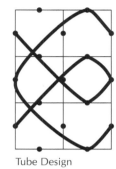

Tube Design

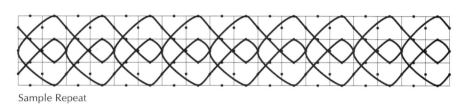

Sample Repeat

Pattern 43 • *Moderate* • 2 tubes

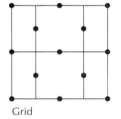

Grid

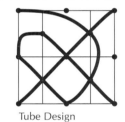

Tube Design

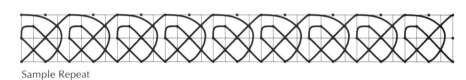

Sample Repeat

Pattern 44 • *Moderate* • 2 tubes

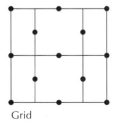

Grid

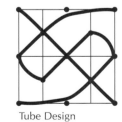

Tube Design

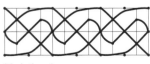

Variation 1

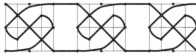

Variation 2

Pattern 45 • *Moderate* • 2 tubes

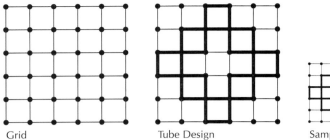

Grid   Tube Design   Sample Repeat

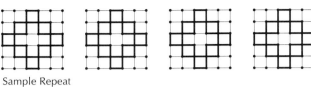

Pattern 46 • *Moderate* • 3 tubes

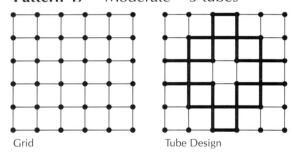

Grid   Tube Design   Sample Repeat

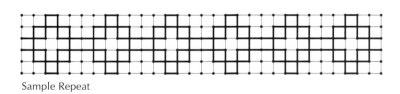

Pattern 47 • *Moderate* • 3 tubes

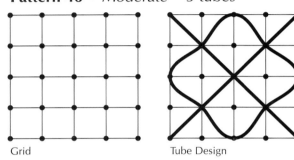

Grid   Tube Design   Sample Repeat

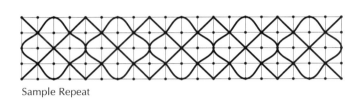

Pattern 48 • *Moderate* • 1 or 2 tubes

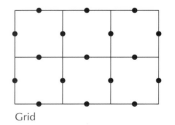 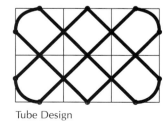

Grid   Tube Design   Sample Repeat

Pattern 49 • *Moderate* • 1 tube

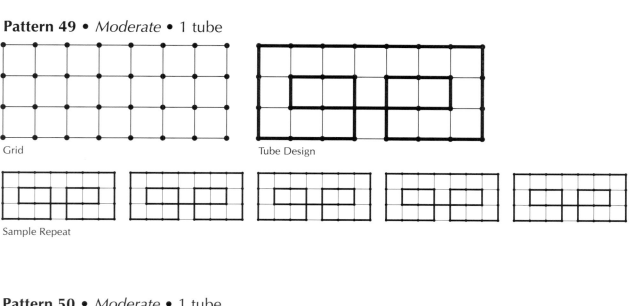

Grid

Tube Design

Sample Repeat

Pattern 50 • *Moderate* • 1 tube

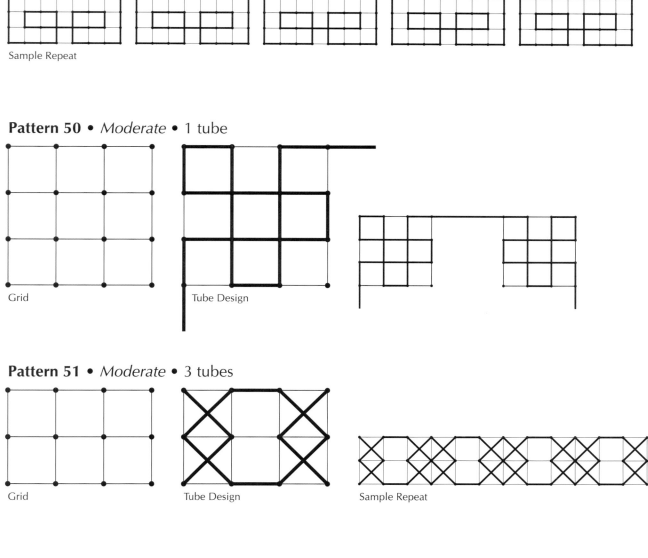

Grid

Tube Design

Pattern 51 • *Moderate* • 3 tubes

Grid

Tube Design

Sample Repeat

Pattern 52 • *Moderate* • 4 tubes

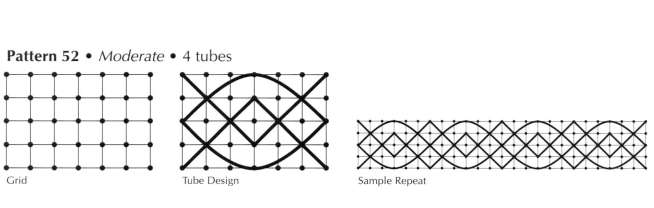

Grid

Tube Design

Sample Repeat

Pattern 53 • *Moderate* • 1 tube

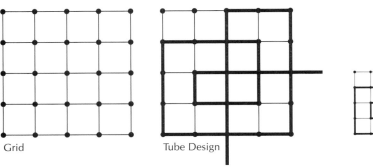

Grid   Tube Design

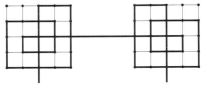

Pattern 54 • *Moderate* • 2 tubes

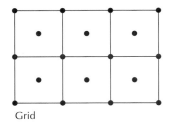 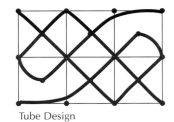 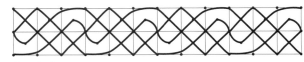

Grid   Tube Design   Sample Repeat

Pattern 55 • *Moderate* • 2 tubes

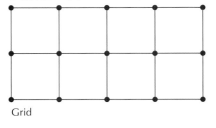 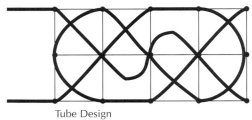

Grid   Tube Design

Sample Repeat

Pattern 56 • *Moderate* • 2 tubes

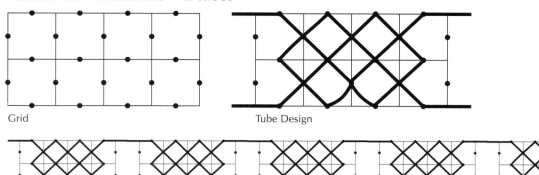

Grid

Tube Design

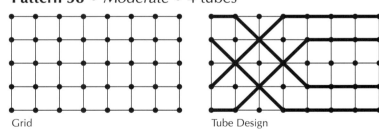

Sample Repeat

Pattern 57 • *Moderate* • 1 tube

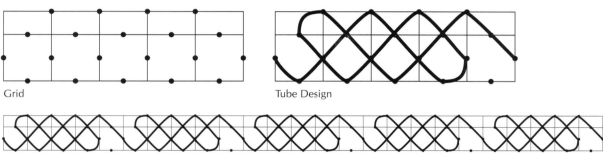

Grid

Tube Design

Sample Repeat

Pattern 58 • *Moderate* • 4 tubes

Grid

Tube Design

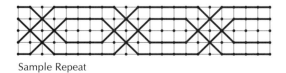

Sample Repeat

Pattern 59 • *Moderate* • 3 tubes

Grid

Tube Design

Variation 1

Variation 2

Pattern 60 • *Moderate* • 2 tubes

Grid

Tube Design

Sample Repeat

Pattern 61 • *Moderate* • 1 tube

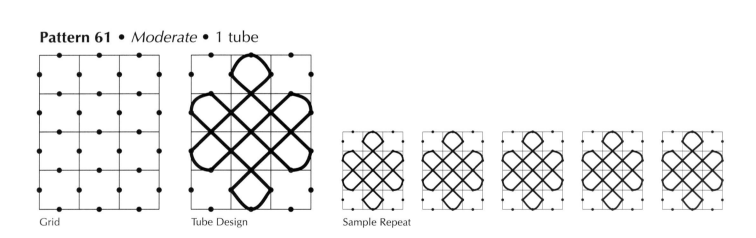

Grid

Tube Design

Sample Repeat

Pattern 62 • *Moderate* • 2 tubes

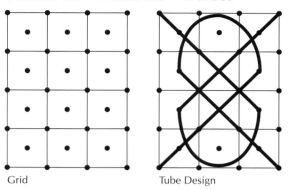

Grid

Tube Design

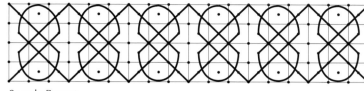

Sample Repeat

Pattern 63 • *Moderate* • 3 tubes

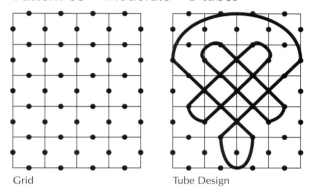

Grid

Tube Design

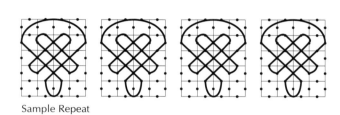

Sample Repeat

Pattern 64 • *Complex* • 2 tubes

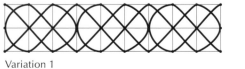

Grid

Tube Design

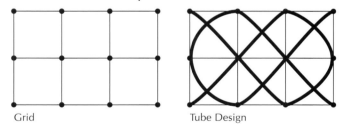

Variation 1

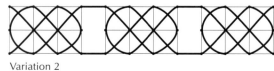

Variation 2

Pattern 65 • *Complex* • 4 tubes*

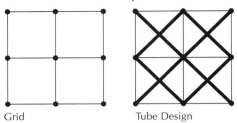
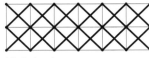

Grid   Tube Design   Variation 1

*When this pattern appears as a separate unit,
 not linked in a series, only 3 tubes are required.

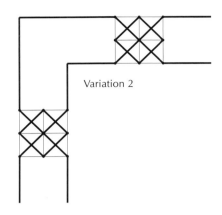

Variation 2

Pattern 66 • *Complex* • 4 tubes

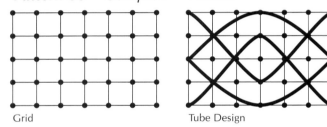

Grid   Tube Design

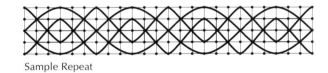

Sample Repeat

Pattern 67 • *Complex* • 3 tubes

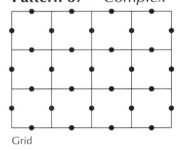

Grid   Tube Design

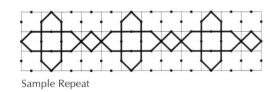

Sample Repeat

Pattern 68 • *Complex* • 1 tube

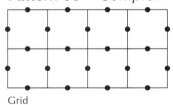
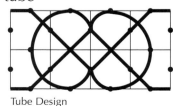

Grid   Tube Design

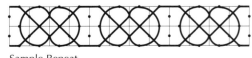

Sample Repeat

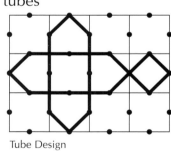

Pattern 69 • *Complex* • 3 tubes

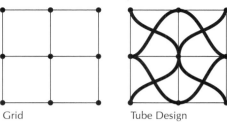

Grid

Tube Design

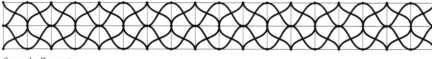

Sample Repeat

Pattern 70 • *Complex* • 2 tubes

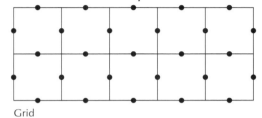

Grid

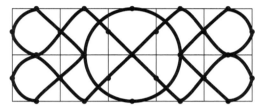

Tube Design

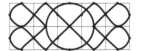    

Sample Repeat

Pattern 71 • *Complex* • 4 tubes

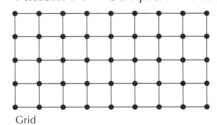

Grid

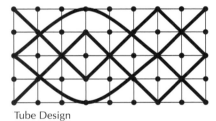

Tube Design

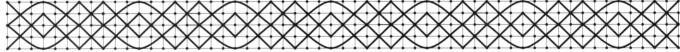

Sample Repeat

Pattern 72 • *Complex* • 4 tubes

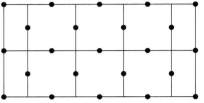

Grid

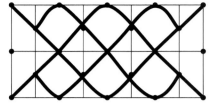

Tube Design

This pattern does not follow the over-under-over-under sequence.
The short tubes must start and end in the under position.
Make up your own sequence of overs and unders;
follow this sequence for each repetition.

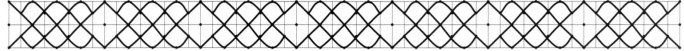

Sample Repeat

Pattern 73 • *Complex* • 2 tubes

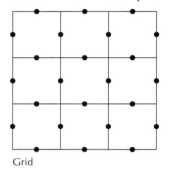

Grid

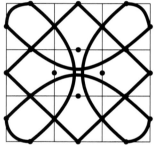

Tube Design

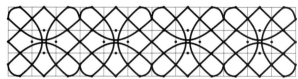

Sample Repeat

Pattern 74 • *Complex* • 4 tubes

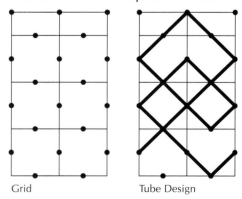

Grid

Tube Design

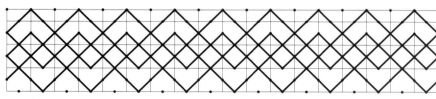

Sample Repeat

Pattern 75 • *Complex* • 2 tubes

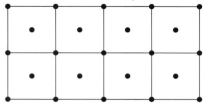

Grid

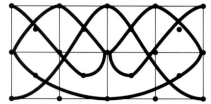

Tube Design

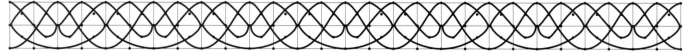

Sample Repeat

Pattern 76 • *Complex* • 4 tubes

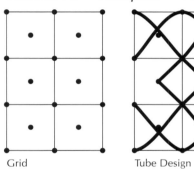

Grid

Tube Design

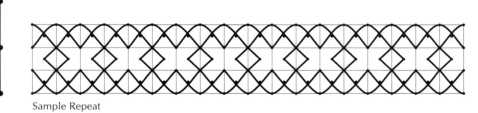

Sample Repeat

Pattern 77 • *Complex* • 3 tubes

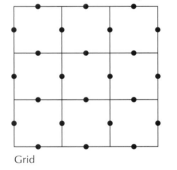

Grid

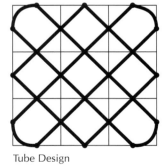

Tube Design

Sample Repeat

Pattern 78 • *Complex* • 2 tubes

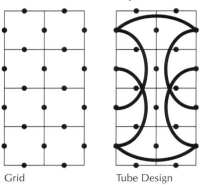

Grid   Tube Design

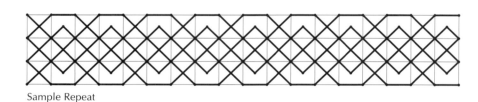

Sample Repeat

Pattern 79 • *Complex* • 6 tubes

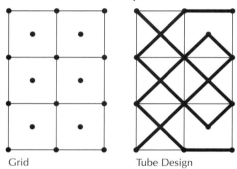

Grid   Tube Design   Sample Repeat

Pattern 80 • *Complex* • 2 tubes

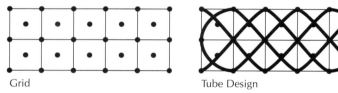

Grid   Tube Design

Variation 1

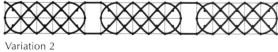

Variation 2

Pattern 81 • *Complex* • 1 tube

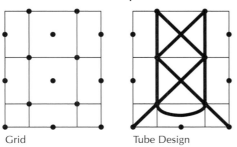

Grid   Tube Design

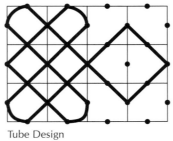

Variation 1

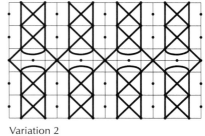

Variation 2

Pattern 82 • *Complex* • 2 tubes

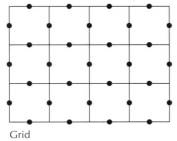

Grid

Tube Design

Sample Repeat

Pattern 83 • *Complex* • 3 tubes

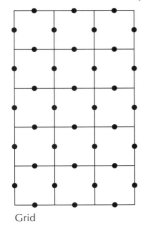

Grid

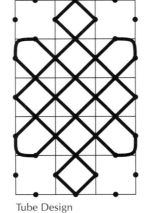

Tube Design

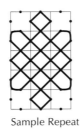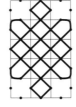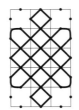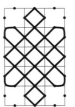

Sample Repeat

Pattern 84 • *Complex* • 1 tube

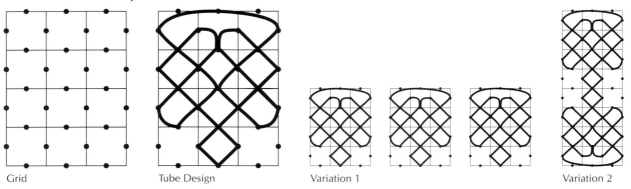

Grid   Tube Design   Variation 1   Variation 2

Pattern 85 • *Complex* • 1 tube

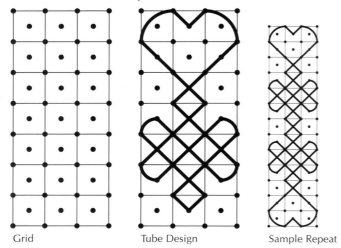

Grid   Tube Design   Sample Repeat

Pattern 86 • *Complex* • 2 tubes

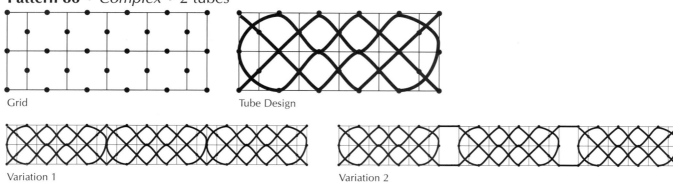

Grid   Tube Design

Variation 1   Variation 2

Pattern 87 • *Complex* • 3 tubes

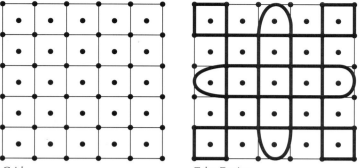

Grid

Tube Design

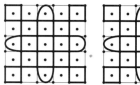 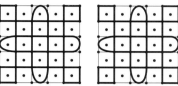

Sample Repeat

Pattern 88 • *Complex* • 1 tube

Grid

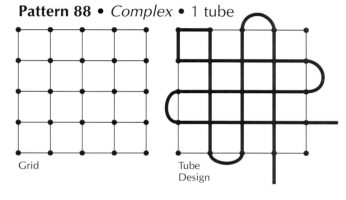

Tube
Design

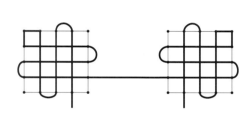

Pattern 89 • *Complex* • 2 tubes

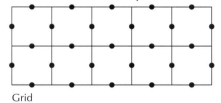

Grid

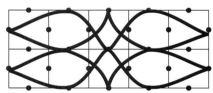

Tube Design

 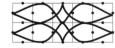 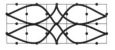 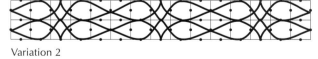

Variation 1

Variation 2

Pattern 90 • *Complex* • 3 tubes

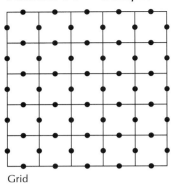

Grid

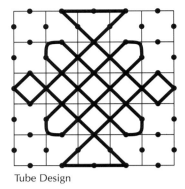

Tube Design

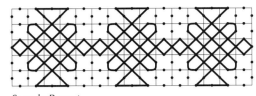

Sample Repeat

Pattern 91 • *Complex* • 2 tubes

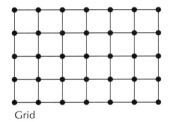

Grid

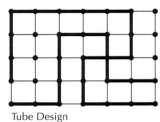

Tube Design

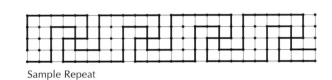

Sample Repeat

Pattern 92 • *Complex* • 1 tube

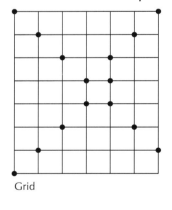

Grid

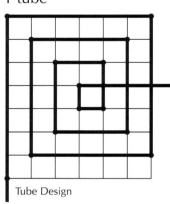

Tube Design

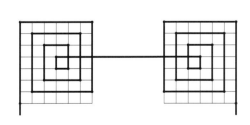

Pattern 93 • *Complex* • 2 tubes

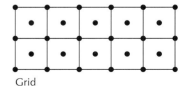

Grid

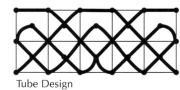

Tube Design

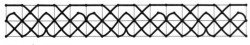

Sample Repeat

Pattern 94 • *Complex* • 4 tubes

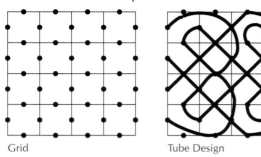

Grid

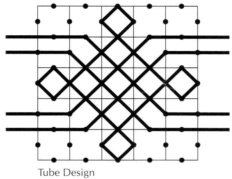

Tube Design

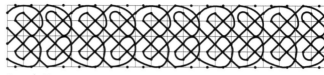

Sample Repeat

Pattern 95 • *Complex* • 5 tubes

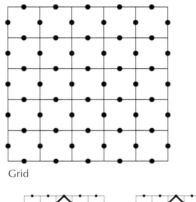

Grid

Tube Design

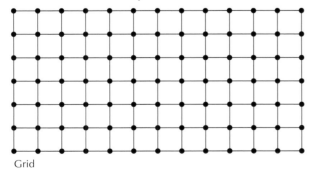

Sample Repeat

Pattern 96 • *Complex* • 4 tubes

Grid

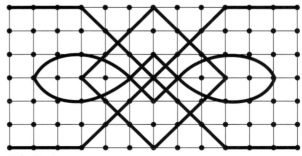

Tube Design

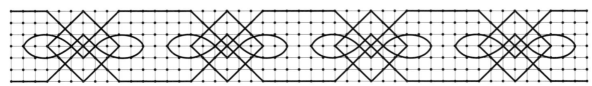

Sample Repeat

Pattern 97 • *Complex* • 3 tubes

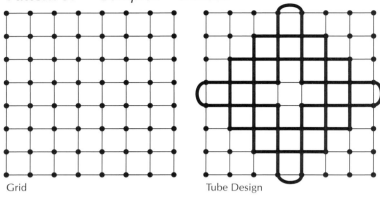

Grid

Tube Design

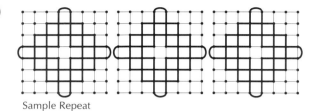

Sample Repeat

Pattern 98 • *Complex* • 4 tubes

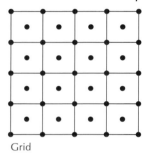

Grid

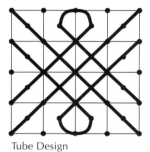

Tube Design

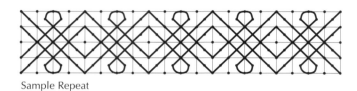

Sample Repeat

Pattern 99 • *Complex* • 6 tubes

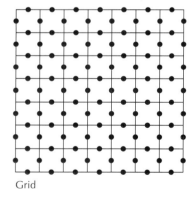

Grid

Tube Design

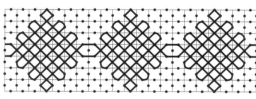

Sample Repeat

Pattern 100 • *Complex* • 4 tubes

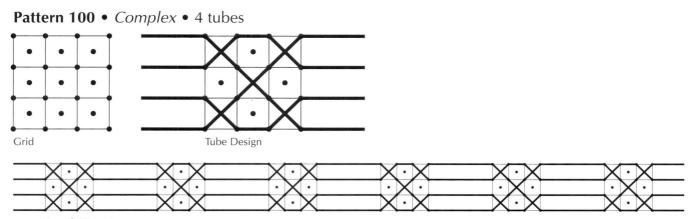

Grid

Tube Design

Sample Repeat

ABOUT THE AUTHOR

As a child, Donna Hussain admired her grandmothers' quilts. But after home economics in junior high school, she vowed never to sew another stitch. Not until her husband's retirement and a move to California in 1989 did she learn to quilt.

In the interim, Donna taught elementary school, collaborated with her professor husband in writing nine computer-science textbooks, lived and traveled abroad during sabbaticals, and raised a son and daughter.

THAT PATCHWORK PLACE TITLES:

AMERICA'S BEST-LOVED QUILT BOOKS®

FIBER STUDIO PRESS TITLES:

PASTIME TITLES:

Many titles are available at your local quilt shop. For more
information, write for a free color catalog to Martingale &
Company, PO Box 118, Bothell, WA 98041-0118 USA.

☎ U.S. and Canada, call **1-800-426-3126** for the name
and location of the quilt shop nearest you.
Int'l: 1-425-483-3313   Fax: 1-425-486-7596
E-mail: info@patchwork.com
Web: www.patchwork.com   6.98